Making Friends

By ine Amos and Annabel Spenceley
nsultant Rachael Underwood

A Cherrytree book

Designed and produced by
A S Publishing

First published 1997
by Cherrytree Press, a division of Evans Publishing Group
2A Portman Mansions
Chiltern St
London W1U 6NR

First softcover edition 1999

Reprinted 2000, 2001, 2002, 2003, 2004

British Library Cataloguing in Publication Data
Amos, Janine
     Making Friends. - (Growing Up)
     1. Friendship - Juvenile literature
     2. Social Interaction - Juvenile literature
     1. Title
     302.1'4

     ISBN 1 84234 006 9

Printed in Malaysia

Ellie and Tom

Splash! It's been raining.

Ellie is jumping in a puddle.

Ellie sees a boy.

"Snap!" says Ellie. "You've got boots on too. You can splash with me."

Tom runs to the puddle.

He jumps with Ellie.

Ellie's mum smiles at them.
"You've made friends," she says.

Danny and Jane

The children are building a house.

Danny is watching.

Danny pushes the blocks.

The house tumbles down.

"Don't do that," shouts Jane. "Now we'll have to build it again."

How do you think Jane feels?
How does Danny feel?

Danny walks away.

Gill the playworker follows him.

"You seem unhappy," says Gill.

"Did you want to play?"

Danny nods his head.

"If you'd like to join in, you can,"
says Gill. "Tell the children what
you want."

"You come too," says Danny.

They go over to the blocks.

"I want to play," Danny says to the children.

"Put some blocks there for the roof,"
Jane tells him.

Danny builds the roof with Jane.

They work together.

Jane smiles at him.
"You're my friend," she says.

How does Danny feel now?

**Sometimes making friends is easy.
You do something together –
and it's fun**

**At other times, you don't know
how to start. If you want to join in,
tell people what you want.
You can find a way to play
together.**